Candy Cigarette

Womanchild Noir

First published 2019 by The Hedgehog Poetry Press

Published in the UK by
The Hedgehog Poetry Press
5, Coppack House
Churchill Avenue
Clevedon
BS21 6QW

www.hedgehogpress.co.uk

ISBN: 978-1-9164806-3-6

9 8 7 6 5 4 3 2 1

A CIP Catalogue record for this book is available from the British Library.

Candy Cigarette

Womanchild Noir

by

Kristin Garth

Contents

Peeler

Chinatown

Pins

Private Dick

Dolls

Invisible Ink

Bracelets

Femme Fatale

You begin a kneeler. Prostrate before two temples,
without crosses just losses, lace collars, buttons
to a collar bone, a menagerie of marigolds
a polyester meadow you hide your demonic design.
You hear it all the time. Whispers/side-eyed
chest glances, inappropriate brief romances
of the mailman/part-time priests, your father's
best friend & him, too. He tells you what to do.
How to close your eyes, to surrender, plead
politely, a little lady, to his higher power
expecting nothing in return for a humble offering
of baby flesh you cannot contain in any Sunday School
dress. You become, for him & in spite of him a

PEELER

There are so many layers he has touched you.
Remove only outermost for other men's money.
The first time you do is baptism of hedonism
& flame. Your skin in neon glistens shame,
five million bonfires inside pores they bore
relentless into your smallest spaces with x-ray eyes.
Yet you're alive. First foray in flames,
a naked new name, it's strange & the same --
a game with rules, tools & fools who feel. Even you.
There are so many layers he has touched you.
It's deeper than clothes, sin & skin.
If you could get to skeleton, maybe you could
begin again & so you peel.

CHEEROTICA

A virgin nerd my senior year, afraid
of boys, ashamed to cheer. Routines remade
in my bedroom in rolled up skirts and braids,
a dad that looms. Fantasy never fades.

I never wore a uniform though plaid's
a princess I adored. A home too bad
for me to stay, a naked nymph nomad
becomes a purchased, pigtailed display.

I dance in kneesocks weekend nights. I shake
my pom-poms under neon lights. Cupcake
cocktails and champagne, a grown up takes
a little name — the only thing I fake.

A topless club that gives this girl so much:
A place I can be me but can't be touched.

PINK PLASTIC HOUSE

The house you buy at 25 is pink
and four feet tall. Twilight Wal-Mart purchase,
you make with cash you mine from men who think
it's all pretend. The pigtails and nervous
titter they believe to be a put-on
the five-inch heels, an ache they think you fake
to take their money. Shake for them till dawn
and buy a plastic puppy, plates heart-shaped
to set a tiny table meant for two.
And it's just you, in kneesocks, hover high
above three stories with something new
to sate the child inside you can't deny.
A plastic house you furnish with pink dreams,
a woman child, exactly what you seem.

BROKEN LITTLE GIRLS

Each Friday night, champagne, a Barbie doll,
the custom ones in Oscar dresses, wide
pink box. Swallowed envy, alcohol,
the only time you can recall you're snide.
"Why not me?" Braids, a Hello Kitty watch,
the one who strips to Barbie Girl, platforms
with bows, kneesocks. A doll each week but not
for you. It's her: red slip, hair jet performs
to Hysteria, Slippery When Wet.
Girlie but gruff, redneck enough to drive
a truck, big wheels, you climb into. She'll set
you straight while eyeliner dries, "I'm like five."
Not the only one in this neon world.
Strip clubs are built from broken little girls.

YOU DON'T WANT THIS

"I don't want this." You're smug in stripes, dark suit.
A table dance turndown with taunt: wry wave,
rebuke my plaid, rebuff my braids. Pursuit:
two pilots, table over — cash, depraved.

A dozen dances, dollars drained. All done,
too damp to dress, my top against my chest,
you suggest, by wave, I stop — lap dance, not shun.
You're bourbon bold — sold, 50, I'm topless.

Pink bubblegum thong grind, your breath behind.
Your smell: savagery, dirt, woods where I hurt
— still want to play. Your thousand offer, declined
for hotel stay. I pout, put on my shirt.

Dark eyes, I'm honest, haunt me to resist.
Weak whisper, but I walk: "You don't want this."

STRIPPING ON 9/11

feels patriotic and this Sisqó song
an anthem, tandem table dances, gift —
two girls for tragedy. Tonight you long
to sacrifice. Work an unscheduled shift
when your house mother calls, explains
"Marines" & you know she means money
then drive beneath a twilight sky, none in air,
to windowless castles to dance for men
in underwear. A topless schoolgirl who
tonight removes the minuscule plaid skirt
she never does because it hides her shame:
potbelly. Drops her pride. Tonight should hurt,
belongs in thongs, America bracelets,
a veteran buys some young service guys
mispronouncing cities where they may die.

IT'S NOT HARD TO PUT A STRIPPER IN CUFFS

for Stormy Daniels

Each county differs, topless or full nude.
The latter you loathe because it also
includes rude house mothers examining pubes.
Law says enough hair there, nothing else shows.
Stand very straight with your knees tightly closed.
You'll hardly move, but you will wear a cape.
Law, not cosplay, no thigh diamond disclosed
behind to frustrate. Super stripper draped
villain by law. A bare nipple is fined
next county. Raw, clear acrylic peels that make
lies true: Didn't see nude. Puritans pine
like Presidents do. They write laws, mistakes for
when they're through (you've been enjoyed enough)
it's not hard to put a stripper in cuffs.

XXX TTY

It's not just him that's on the phone. He's deaf,
this customer. You should have known. He types
to you, TTY, translated request
by some young jocular guy. Sounds like snipes
what he relays — the pay, full nude, where you
will meet the boat Sunday. A birthday gift
you said you'd never be — and naked, too;
ignoring boundaries. Just topless shifts
inside the bar. No outside dances, nude,
with caviar. Your boss insisted for
her friend, executive, distinguished, lewd
   "a gentleman — just one hour, nothing more."
But this witness, because it's TTY,
knows how expensive you are to buy.

ENTERTAINERS

They play the Beastie Boys. He says let's dance.
The "let's" implies all — you, him, stranger stuck,
all rayon sweat slunk pleather couch. Askance
dark irised other jiggling man tits, sucked
to sleep tonight, his baby concubine
if you obey this signal, strip for two
more men. It's Friday night, the hundredth time,
at least, for you — an entertainer, too,
like him, a guitar player. Consider
a Jimmy Page analogy, his hotel
room post concert when the other stripper
asked him to play and he said *bloody well
just did.* He'd just hear the hotel. Think whore.
It's better if you don't say anymore.

BROOM

They speak websites, ignore, in black and white,
brunette exsanguinated tv mute
receptacle you can't unsee. Her tight
perfected v of thigh, the yogic brute
solidity of pose — fingered calves, sky
high, a dancer — you the pigtailed girl
abused next door variation. Some spry
pike driven deep into dark curls
slick pubic hair, an offscreen strong-armed ghost,
bald back of head in frame now with a brush,
contextual clue — broom. You loom engrossed
her fate already photographed. No rush,
to flee, live girl, they summoned here to dance.
You're doomed. You wait for it, by broom, entranced.

PLAID KITTEN

A kitten written wanton, bad but smiles
so meek in skirts of plaid. Charcoal, crimson
intersects a schoolgirl demeanor, wiles
with kinky sex. Blue black outlined yellow sun,
shy smiles inside the darkness done. In cream
criss-cross on mottled sage, she pouts, a pig-
tailed Betty Page. Turquoise gingham, daydream
pristine, a freckled cheek, deceitful gig
obscene. A tartan twirl to thrill in twill,
stiletto crawl towards the tallest stack
of bills — a dollhouse, alone, tattersall,
flared skirt so small, your heart attacked
is bitten, smitten; across a lap, she purrs
a ruby clawed outlaw, pervert demure.

UNBOUND

Redemption in black opal eyes, ribald,
in rags yet recognized: her chestnut curls
and pearlescent thighs. Story, scars and barbs
anthologized before she was a girl.

Ramshackle mansion castle made. A stone
staircase to onyx tiara displayed
atop a shelf of ebony. A throne
he crafted when she is three, midnight brocade.

He wrote you in a gothic book. A girl
so regal, world's mistook, debased to dance
without her clothes. A naked twirl
a perfect princess shows — surreal romance.

A tiny mistress in a strip club found,
from page to stage, a novel love unbound.

You leave the beach. They wanted you to teach &
you did as Puritans prescripted, directed
at least for a second – or a year then crossed a bridge
to Pensacola towards autonomy & topless cheers.
You peel five years, a trillion tears, two apartments
& a house, two feline ghosts (arson & leukemia) whose
haunts is close and quiet, as a mouse. Arson, one more
time, true crime is let inside your little life. An atheist,
for you, leukemia is criminal, new – scientific, insoluble.
Disease is Manson, Bundy, Bateman without a fury or a
face. You feel displaced. Not in Pensacola at all – instead
maybe a movie & you have found your way inside of it.
It's you, Faye & Jack, directed through iconic noir
frames by a pedophile. Pensacola is just a movie called

CHINATOWN

which if you could get out of it, you will tell everyone
means rigged deal, a never changing nightmare of rich
monster fathers who make women into screechers
of truths that take two hours to decipher like: daughter is sister.
Two hours to untangle trauma that, for a woman,
is biology & life. In Chinatown, it is daughter/sister.
In Pensacola, it is daughter/wife. A slip of lips from broken
hips, so high on morphine, he'll say it to an emergency
room doctor. "This is my wife," & it will be you, his
oldest daughter. A noir revelation to a doctor you save
from Chinatown, a shake of a head & a smile. It is your
style. He's a do-gooder with hearts & hips to heal.
One right now. He doesn't need to know he lives in
Chinatown, & he won't. Doesn't even live, like you,
in Pensacola. At least not today.

TALKING TO A TEENAGE GIRL ABOUT HER MOUTH

The dentist says you're biting me again.
You're not, but laughing gas, fingers, tools
prohibit speech. Your mouth is held open.
He fills a cavity. His voice is cool,
impatient when he says next, wider, though
your jaw is aching, stretched, small, childlike
as your height, limbs. It's something that he knows.
Hygienists use child dental trays despite
your age because you haven't yet outgrown
that baby mouth — but he is hurt. He says
(some years, for you, before his meaning's known)
you'll make some man very unhappy one day.
His hygienist blinks and looks, from you, away.
She understands. You will, too, one day.

14 AND KNEELING FOR A
JV DEFENSIVE LINE COACH

your pre-algebra teacher, middle aged
who's flanked with teenage letter jacket sweat
of three, your age — the compulsion, green page
before your knees, khaki berber. you let
it drop, midterm report, its red-inked D
provokes this plea — some extra credit? can't
bring home below a c because he beats
you now, your father. this desperate rant
compressed, confessed secrets minutes between
this class, the next, distressed. he says "beg me."
they slip from lips, the words but he says "knees,"
and you'll appease while three smile, snicker — see
how quick you move despite the way you feel.
they learn you are a girl they can make kneel.

PEEPHOLES

She learns it all through peepholes, the way
you do when you're a girl. Like whispers sly
as uncle's lurid giggles, things they say
about the taste of girls, her age, down by
the river, like she isn't even there. She spies
through slats in closets, unicorns, a gift
a balding man bequeaths a teen and lies
about its purity. A horned horse grift
between her fingers, key of glass to where
the girls are dealt like cards and disappear.
Their dealer all in black, the coldest stare
between riddle, reproof: "The owner's here."
In bed, she waits for truth this place imparts.
Her daddy comes to claim his queen of hearts.

NAILBITER

The consequence of bitten lips, frequent
sanguine sacrificial feasts, fingertips,
ten nails all nibbled, virgin bed, discreet
ceremonial female bloodshed. Drips
defile a Laura Ashley dress. Secret-
keeper, costumed to confess daintily,
safe sins, her own, misdemeanors. The rest,
suppressed, swallowed alone. Guilt — a lady
in garnet gloves, sonambulating speech
hallucinating blood — is palmistry,
teenage hands, ouroboros the meek
may understand — abuse anxiety.
In floral patterned innocent pretense,
her fingernails are bloody evidence.

MILK TEETH

no longer
her subsistence crumbs
ancient hunger
starvation young.
animal you make
mincemeat.
what's bottle fed
forgets its teeth.
milk teeth malformed,
affable, a grotesquerie
naive, a little laughable.
student turned to succulent,
who soaks & sucks,
who you forget.
candy apple,
two lips, a tongue,
hollowed out
for secrets young.
a shiny shell
with worm beneath,
blue gingham dress,
red underneath.
a head you hold,
your rosebud wish;
her bite you stole
just like her kiss.

YOUR HUSBAND DRIVES ME HOME

The years I babysit, I cannot drive.
Dad's plan to keep me both alive & safe
wretched, in-waiting wife & waif. Deprive
me of any temptation or mistake —
protect a virtue, his prerogative
to take, like trust. I'm 18, older men,
like him, eyeballing lace outlines furtive,
pretending to listen, requisition
movements of lips with questions, suggestions
of syllables before wives audition,
midnight date night teenage assignation
inside of cars compliant & conditioned.
There is not a man who leaves me alone,
but you will have your husband drive me home.

YOUR BODY IS HIS BLESSING

You cry at 20, waitress brings a 12
& under menu. Parents laugh. "You're blessed.
You'll see." Dad should believe in blessings. Self
appointed prophet, from god a bequest
of daughters honor him. You the eldest
bequeathed his childlike face, his taste for what
will singe hot pink insides of lips, closest
expression of his own eyes chestnut.
stay small, full grown except those breasts
attests your status — reflection & toy
consecrated to him first then the rest.
He means you are a thing men will enjoy,
endorsement you are built to be possessed.
This body has never made you feel blessed.

EXPERIMENT

Beneath sadistic guys -- bulging eyes, thin
slit grind, slick twinges tickling my veins
tormenters never see. A frog so thin
sea green, dead that I no longer strain
against gloved hands — an easy pry, my limbs
to open legged, synthetic splendor. Posed
then poked, and then that magic crack of whim-
infested bone turns dangle, all flexed toes.
A dozen scientific eyes — each tries
to say their fingers aren't the ones that flip
the switch, compel my naked corpse to writhe
and spread, undead, lab table bed, last glimpse
of what they knew a year ago or more —
electric, death-defying little whore.

AN ENTRANCE IS NOT AN EXIT

16 is sacrifice. Serpents seek skin.
Sequestration a season, and then they
begin — reptilian gazes, demon
enchantment, sheepskin, diabolists who crave
consumption within. You are an entrance.
Composition is doors, all orifices,
indefensible pores. Not much hindrance,
loose locks, their lizard tongues, biramous,
shared skeleton keys. Annihilation,
your gender, seems conspiracy. Your deal
with devils when dying is gestation,
a cannibal new just hunger you feel.
An entrance no exit, you let them in
a cemetery inside teenage skin.

You are pieces positioned -- a puzzle
perdition, permitted & licensed, Pensacola
peeler, lithe, liquid confidence & natural tits,
you dance, legit, before demons, dark-suited
eloquence amidst ex-college linebackers,
Cyclopean focus of bouncers, six hours:
six inches of space the law demands
between a seated, suited body & a naked
one that writhes, back bent & stands, the
hocus pocus of hands, whispered table dance
demands. By breasts, you're blessed this topless
tenure along with your braids – but success is
something south, styled & socked in fishnets,
argyle, lacey ankles & cotton white midnight climb
towards a thigh that ends below places you bend:

PINS

You're short, but this sport's a stilettoed charade
a mainstage parade of diminutive maids.
Their pieces positioned, a puzzle taken apart,
you learn the value of peeled pieces even a heart.
Your breasts passed their tests - your chest
photographed by a peer, emulated by a surgeon,
so some nights they appear & shake the same,
a man-made mirror on someone else's chest.
Two pieces essential, but lower is best.
They rest upon shoulders. They're dressed
in garters & green. In unicorns & hearts,
your innocence is obscene. Depletion
of dollars, hollers, they spend, decoration
of Benjamins collected on a womanchild's pins.

SOCK SLUT

Two legs, in ponies prancing, strut, a chest
of socks that won't quite shut, a maxed
out Visa cruel clerks can cut. Stripe of flesh,
thigh high, argyle smut — a cotton climax.

A stalk of stores and styles galore — Target,
princess, Wal-mart, whore. No kneesocks left in
her hometown. Safari hunts requisite
for pairs unfound, such snug secrets on skin.

Pictures, poses, provocateur, she talks
to strangers young, mature. Photo shoots
in heels and bed with socks on arms and bows
on head, acrylic paisley prostitute.

Be it addiction or stylistic rut,
her game is gams, no shame; her name: sock slut.

AGAIN

"Again" is all he says to you. Thigh high
black socks, a kitchen counter stage strip show
reveal, moth-pallor calves, a cross-legged thigh,
pink plaid sneak peek half heart of ass. The glow
across your kitchen, amber, ash he drops,
defiles your tile. Hands occupied, up/down
movements, slow peel, surreal, of socks. He stops
you with "again." Hour he strokes, smokes. He frowns —
you wouldn't dare. You're barely even there,
untouchable beguiler, baby faced
displaced once teacher/girlfriend material
a topless occupation has erased.
Your countertop in tears, but you'll pretend
that this is what you want to do again.

FISHNET NOIR

I cast my net, an onyx diamond stretch,
a thigh in jet. A pour of milk inside
a sieve velvet with holes your fingers catch,
a perfect pet who purrs but cannot hide.
Your touch a threat, a rip I won't regret
released to sweat and writhe, for you,
not forget who's vanquished in this vignette.
And once I'm wet, no trouble to subdue,
a bound brunette, my flesh expressed in mesh,
a trap you tame, your only tool a pole.
My dominant who rips his way to flesh,
a tear, adept, you trace me hole by hole.
Unravel, erect, an eager silhouette
of girl in net, no secrets from you kept.

VORTEX

In pigtails, small town skies of gray, you thought
that you could run away from witches, rules
and negativity. Already caught,
you cannot see. Until the vortex —cruel
it seems — knocks you into gingham dreams.
Blue socks, sabbatical, patchwork bedspread,
villainy flies, tyrannical screams,
in freckled head. By mesmerism led
to cyclone, black magic you give a home —
her poppy field becomes a bed. Broomstick,
she's watching overhead. By you alone
invented witch. From bike to flight, a trick
of sorcery, your cerebral cortex,
inside innocence, evil and vortex.

THE SCARLET SOCKS

They're kept inside a velvet box. Bijou
the key, bitty, burgundy lock. A chain
of silver near a pious throat subdues
sublime this sin sunlight eschews. She's pain
in public, diabolical dark eyes.
Small strokes of key stokes thoughts of thighs.
From pulpit, pew, a cheeky wink surprise.
Of scarlet socks, you fantasize. So shy
at midnight, feather bed, unbuttoned, bare,
long legs in red. Across your lap, her flesh
aflame, a vermillion temptress who wears
your shame. Her crimson climax, she'll confess.
In twill, a demon, worsted, doll depraved
you save. In scarlet socks, she will behave.

THE SECRET OF THE SOCKS

You strip five years. They never see a toe.
Elongated prophetic second
you hide since an ill-fated playground show --
a schoolgirl sandaled circle beckons
inside. You're naive. In kitty flip flops,
sunshine, smiling like you're normal. Pride
before the pointing prophesy stops
you — educated by despot. You cried,
believed predictions, second grade redhead
oracle, speaks it clear, smug sneer, "It means
you will be bigger than your husband." Said
& seen, your second toe the only lean
offender in this space. From then to pole,
you hide shame in socks — never show a sole.

HITCHHIKER

Sun sluiced snowflakes, honey hair,
suitcase, her race to anywhere.
Staircase, tiptoes 18th birthday
escape to anyplace distinct, far away.
Change of clothes, a cherry glitter gloss,
a paperback, a raw romantic loss,
platforms, grey socks above the knee,
resolve to not come back,
a haphephobic family.
Walks for days on blistered feet.
The road is hell, demons replete,
finger service, wet lips, in driver's seat.

KNEESOCK CODE

When they are pink, I giggle, wink and bounce.
Your knee becomes a slide to lap I ride
to ecstasy my dimpled cheeks announce.
My socks a sign a child still hides inside.

When they are black, I crave attack, demon
demands, disgrace so dark my own's displaced --
your horns & porn, secrets eaten
off hardwood floors, a beast who begs for bones.

Above the knee, a map, a swath of skin
you long to slap. From pale to pink, so slick
between bare thighs, I punctuate so prim
with pointed toes, your arrow erotic.

A cotton couple little heart unlocks:
Desire deciphered in a choice of socks.

A courtesan in cinnamon -- a red hot Valentine
lipstick outline of the girl you've been -- a little
lust, a little blood, a trickle, lost, who has found
the flood. Patrimony, your new estate, around a
phallic backlit stage, the progeny await. A babydoll
they rent awhile, pink champagne, pristine schoolgirl
style, they want you because they see your need
even mottled, muddled with pink glitter, greed –
a cocktail of feelings when you're peeling for
them, a roomful of wishes in the shape of old men,

SUGAR DADDIES

young ones, too, you crave in your sleep, a cradle,
a bottle, a promise they'll keep. You rotate their tables
a dozen some nights, hide your hunger & hatred too
fierce to fight. You want them to save you, to take you
away. You know exactly what words you should
say. You want to live in their laps, but you'll push
them away. You think you could love them, but you
want them to pay. Dozens of daddies diametrically aged.
You like it that way – securing your wage. Always a spare,
when one goes astray. Perpetually happens, they all do some
day -- to their wife or their life, a co-worker with little
to say, smaller or taller, a smile that asks them to play.
It's a strip club remember. They don't have to care.
They get what they want, what they pay for –
lemonade hair, pink lollipopped miniscule underwear.
You'll grind on another like you don't even care
but without even peeking know they are aware.
Waterproof mascara can only contains so many tears
so many years of collected, curated pain. It's what is
explained in red-veined, kohl smudged eyes – what
smiles & twirls cannot disguise – it gives you away
what falls from your eyes. They see it -- the psychologist
client, many less educated, informally wise –
the wet evidence you are a thing that still feels.
It's not just those breasts you reveal that are real.
You're one of the few they will ever see cry.
They can still woo & wound you & man will they try.

VERUCA WANTS

She wants a ticket made of gold — to be
the first whose fingers hold what Daddy finds
with workers, poor, peanut shellers, weary,
a wrapper-littered warehouse floor. Confined
five days, unwrapping bars. Her hysterics
have them seeing stars. Smudges chocolate,
hundreds of hands all servants to esoteric
adolescent demands: a world in pocket,
a golden goose, pink macaroons, some trained
baboons, ten thousand tons of ice cream. Men
who'll jump before she screams. Her Daddy's drained,
depleted, nut tycoon, a shell worn thin.
He hears her — even in his dream she haunts;
nightmares: tomorrow, what Veruca wants.

CANDY CIGARETTES

The tragedy of us — inside we're twelve.
My candy cigarette chainsmoke, pinstripe bespoke
your suit, convenience store, costumed noir. Delve
into your pocket, frigid Slurpee poke,
of fingertips, a teen detective caught,
before I have a clue, cherry-handed —
receipt/poetic benediction sought,
pickpocket your mystery. Remanded
always empty handed, to prison bars,
wide stripes. Two adolescent archetypes:
teen femme fatale, a private dick with scars
consigns me criminal, stereotype:
you lock inside with juvenile regrets,
a begger you bring candy cigarettes.

AMBITION

You liked her lemonade stand. You take it
in hand. You speak like a daddy so that
she'll understand. Her girlification
of your business plan — will not read what
is written. Taste. Demand. Push pennies at
her — grime, black residue. Sunshine beneath,
a glint — cute, squinched — of you. Placate
with pats, promise offhand. Sharp teeth
bequeath; good girls understand. You're all plans,
wingtips, projects to do; her saccharine
empire eclipses you. You own the land.
You burn her sign, her stand now ash once pine.
Simplify her, something small to amuse —
ambition's just ammunition you use.

HALF OF HIS HEART

for Half of My Heart by John Mayer featuring Taylor Swift

Sundress, success, eyelet empress, birdcaged
antiqued teenage regrets, tiptoe koi pond condo
Twitterverse. A fingered heart stage
romance, your ritual rehearsed. A wand
your words yield you sunflower fields. You wield
with whimsy, glockenspiel. Soliloquies
in microphones, the flesh outline reveals
the hole alone. Cute ambition, he sees
in you — a lavender lemonade, and
he's thirsty, too. You're pop on blues,
your dress his chess, some backup vocals stand-
in Stevie Nicks request. You can't refuse.
Your body of work? Your body in part?
Why does he want you? Which half of his heart?

RED LICORICE, BLACK LINGERIE

Black lingerie, red licorice, pink lust
in lace you trace then kiss. Delight inside
a dark doe eye. A freckled cheek is just
an alibi. I'm neither virgin, bride
in white. I'm looking for a dirty knight.
I'm not a child — not naive. Educate
me. Make me believe. Girl who's erudite
enough: my filth is Faulkner; sex, soulmate
are rough. I like a man to hold me down.
I'll struggle, but I'll never frown. A fuck's
a frolic, fishnet affair; pigtails, a crown,
ribbons I'll wear — what brings me licks and luck.
Both rough and sweet right now as yesterday;
buy me red licorice, black lingerie.

BLOW POP LOVE

I taste, in you, my teens, a skinny stick
I pull from jeans. Unwrap a scarlet dome
so dry, a shell I salivate to lick
and lubricate. Your ridges tongued become
a cherry smooth until undone. A bulge
between teeth and cheek graduates too soon
to sucks. Can't wait for what's within, indulge
an ever childish mind, surprise balloon
of pink behind a candied veneer. Roof
I rub to raw with rhythmic thrusts to get
to what's inside. My bubble lust reproof
deflates you to a tasteless wax secret.
You're sucked not savored since I was a child.
I still race through tastes that make me smile.

DOMESTICATED ANIMUS

I'm pigtails in your dirt, a woman you
can hurt. An ambush in the plains remade
romantic rooftop rut against a flue
of brick. Your sick suggestions my legs splayed
so slick, such sentiments conveyed. A pet
you let off leash to lunge, a little, roam,
midnight inside a plastic park. Swingset
assignations after dark then bring me home:
a blanket and a bone. An animal
your own, once prey you tackled, trained, renamed
not tame behind discreet suburban walls.
This animus domestic unrestrained,
a gingerbread McMansion underneath
two predators who haven't lost their teeth.

So slick & quick, they always start. They know
each ventricle of a schoolgirl's heart, pretenders,
naked, just like you, with lesson plans & homework,
too. Summons, secret, to a bed to play. No strip
club required. They will not pay for a bookish
girl they've known for years, before the days
of topless cheers – coquettish in a velvet dress,
punk rock bar, a college girl they pushed too far.
The one who moved you from your parents' house,
first smoke, first choke, first heart cut out to Jane's
Addiction, red face, low lights & sweat tell you all you
should have already known. He's not alone. He's a

PRIVATE DICK

different than the ones who pay, seek lust & love
in a public, prescripted way. They make the rules.
They know who you are. You can try to change
a made-up mind, but you won't get too far. They
know all your details. They calculate their words.
Their histories are mysteries. Every last stand, line
in the sand is buried & blurred. They look at you
sometimes, a blank stare you recognize -- the cool
calculations of a predator's eyes. You've seen it
in mirrors, some nights at the club when some
out-of-town businessman has fallen in love. He's speaking
of somedays, a dream that necessitates you, and you're
counting how many more table dances you need to do
to buy a TV as big as your friends. How many more
twerks & how many bends? In public, a private dick
will preen, a pile of pretty words on display. In
private, you'll see it. He will make you pay.

PREDITOR

An editor, you choose "organic" when
explaining, to me, how we happened. Like
I'm fruit, plucked, backwoods vine, from thorns. Swells, skin
storm-soaked, seared, southern summer berry ripe
enough to tumble for a moment on
a poet's tongue before bicuspids tear
bruised exocarp to ooze, undone
to dregs — delicious residue despair.
In truth, you met me in a magazine —
dysfunction with details, abuse outlined
in rhyme, pigtailed photo, poem obscene;
schoolgirl perfect for homework you'd assign.
You use the language of an editor.
You chose a body like a predator.

HALF-FINISHED HOUSES

Half-finished houses are suburban caves
you pull me in to misbehave. A will-
be window arch, the sawdust fresh shaved,
invites trespass midnight, slab initialed,
a small of back engraved. You kick away
the nails, the two by four, debris. Open
me where they will watch TV, and you say
in whispers "welcome home" — one more broken
thing you will never own. Wandering streets,
found, just like me — new construction, exposed
circuitry. Timorous in plastic sheets,
I am beneath you, deflowered, bulldozed.
You will find another when this one's through.
You like unfinished things to wander through.

PRIMITIVE

Incantation, a secret beach, inside
me under seagull squeaks. They circle in
a cyan sky then alight alongside,
to lock black eyes with mine. On cheek and chin,
adornments powdered sand. My small of back,
you steer with primitive hands. Whispers, miles,
this prehistoric place, across train tracks,
a barricade breached; time's erased. Defiled
before I'm on the ground; winged witnesses
whose squawks with moans resound. Most ancient, wild
animal noise, archaeopteryx
the dialect employed. Prohibited
this lust outside where we're still primitive.

EVEN ASSHOLES GET TO BE ANONYMOUS

You hit a bottom — what they say it takes
to know you're not okay. Find a program,
two initials; last one is A. To make
the circle round this room, brand new, goddamn
nervous, too, stripper at a church — not there
to pray. To find another way. To say
before a room of strangers that you bare
your breasts for money, and you woke in a
drug dealer's bed last Saturday. It scared
you here. To them. To him, the leader, near,
who calls you poison, stare fixed square
against your tits. It's drugs that brought you here.
You thought you hit your bottom in a bed.
You find it in a church basement instead.

LUNAR MATH

I'm bad at math, a bit better in bed
inside a Hello Kitty gown, a pulled
midnight comforter, should be asleep instead
staring at an indecipherable
moon, coy shapeshifter in the trees. Like you,
it could be slivers or a half— never all
of anything. Distant reflection skewed
through branches, dancing orbit of eyeballs
its tease, nightly, illumination,
self revelation. Beaming enough before
retreating I'm inventing equations,
the emotional calculus of whores,
to make your impossible trip again,
footprint barren surfaces I descend.

NECROPOLIS

You gained admittance like a ghost. Gashed gauze
of girlishness; it tore you, too, almost.
Transmuted flesh to memory, a sawed-
off sympathy inside my innermost
necropolis of buried flesh — mound
of bones without an exodus. Mass grave,
marauders, matchstick men, communal sounds
of summoning in skin. You sought to save
me for yourself, to exorcise what haunts
my mental health, my hollows where you float
& hide — your human residue of wants
reside. A sarcophagus devoted,
yours alone, renovated while you roam,
a haunted brothel made vacation home.

A MAP OF PINECONES

I ran away from you into the wild.
You taught the appellations of each tree.
I made a map of pinecones as a child.
Beneath your apparition is banshee.

I sprinkle dirt to cover where I tread.
I learned from you the danger of a trail,
the compass of a body that has bled.
Survival's skeleton is small details.

I make my flesh into a mystery —
my pallor painted, freshly showered earth.
Retreat is careful choreography.
You must not smell the memory of hurt.

Hold shut the wounded places you defiled.
I will not let you find me in the wild.

KRISTINS

In Pensacola, you attract a boy
who breaks his house arrest to come attack
you on your parents' couch. After, annoys
you by discussing former Kristins that
he screwed, one used to live for years right down
your street. You shared a gym, a blonde, performed
the uneven bars so well her mom found
a better coach and sent her off. He's scorned
because she doesn't want dealers in bed
with her prize child, even if he went to Deerfield --
a temper taken out on you instead.
Invites you home, all glass in woods. His floor,
third story, looks down on trees like he does you.
He makes you bleed. You focus on the view.

GOOD GIRL GONE

You know that it is over when you go
to see him after midnight, dressed
in babydoll pajamas the breeze blows
up on your way inside. Think how impressed
he'll be with such a cheeky surprise. Use
your key and climb in bed, the place he should
be but isn't, his "early night," a ruse.
You know what it must mean; it isn't good.
You leave ashamed his neighbors will get a view
of you, this needy whore without a clue.
For him, you were a good girl, pure and true,
and look at where it's fucking gotten you.

KITTEN SMITTEN

December starving, throat yowled mute, big eyes
beside his garbage chute; he picks you up,
in just one hand, pinstriped, bowtied,
a civilized man. His warm fingers cup
you scruff & bones, a stunted youth he thinks
he owns. A baby beast he takes to train —
emaciated, broken brain. You slink
inside his ordered life, penthouse constrained
feral child wife with claws he files & paints
pale pink, instincts he hopes become extinct:
predation, fornication, chewed through restraints,
ingratitude & nude complaints. Your blink
& thighs belie the fangs, you hide, full grown.
He would have let you starve if he had known.

NIPPLE

Pulls you to his chest, after all the rest
to fall asleep the way that he desires.
you suckling his right nipple like a breast.
"Like you are starving, and it can make milk."
Its slight erection tight between your lips
because you know it's true. He does feed you,
something more than the mimicked milk this tit,
diminutive, cannot express.   A coup
to keep it in until he's snoring but,
if you do, it makes you, in fact, his child,
a babydoll undressed then nursed. It's what
makes it okay that he hurts you — defiles
then feeds. Both father, mother, he can be.
He knows how much you need a family.

Schoolgirl strippers sleep alone — 3 am Waffle House
hashbrowns before, maybe, a bone, sometimes, if you have
the drive — a little hornier than sleep deprived. Exhaustion
usually sets in. It's more manual labor for a womanchild
perpetually between boyfriends. Your thighs are taut, cramped
with pain - too many backbends, too much overpriced cheap
essential champagne. Pensacola's a place that ends at 2:00 a.m.,
the public parts where lust begins. It's 4, for you, when workday
becomes play. All normies asleep, sorted, shorn sheep, snoring,
this late even on a Saturday. The ones awake have vampire jobs
like you, bartenders, musicians, men who deal drugs are just off
work & ready, too -- seeking something new that isn't love. Some
twilight glitter tight inside a glove. It's a stripper thing. Men don't
see you. They believe the pantomime of pornography you do.
A peeler risqué is risky to touch. It's said, silent smug faces,
so many nights, the site makes you not want them much. You have
the pity of kitties, two, alive at different times. Between their
lives & deaths, you seek something small you can call mine. You
have hundreds & even if they're plastic, painted, pretend, hard &
cold, you will still hold your

DOLLS

They are different-aged babies waiting for you. Their eyes always
open and focused, an unblinking beatific light blue. Not dark like
your own filled with danger & dirt - a cavernous stare hollowed
by heredity, hatred & hurt. They mimic innocence perfect & new.
You study vacuous vinyl faces & emulate their pristine particulars,
too. It makes you money, a smile that won't end. You drive after to
Wal-Mart and spend some on them - furniture, dresses, socks and
shoes for their feet. It's a deal that you make with the part of you inside
that stays sweet - the child in the woman who you sell every night.
She lets you do it, but you know inside it's not right. Even if
she isn't, by chronology, she hurts likes a child princess in a palace-
shaped sex shop she shouldn't be. It's her face that slays them; it's
her heart they cut. It's her pain she swallows to get what you want.
She's small still inside you. She is human & raw, but you wear her
image for dollars like she is just some inanimate doll.

PLASTIC HEADS

An arm chair Daddy dead for days, a week
of whispered Barbie fingerplays. Assumed
asleep until the smell, her grief, that stink,
just plastic heads to tell. Decay that looms,
a house in hay, no human help for miles
away. Her friends, they fit on fingertips
with hair that glitters, lacquered lips. Their smiles
transport her, yellow bus, with voices, scripts
so treacherous. And when one's bad, she's sent
to bed, a flick of finger to forehead.
A rolling rebel's quick brunette descent
empties a finger for a blonde instead.
What lives inside her comes from what is dead.
A heavy heart invents a plastic head.

BABYDOLL

I'm baptized with my babydoll. I grow
but change not much at all. A ribbon in
synthetic hair, two blinky eyes follow
me everywhere — a mother pretend.

Barbie-brainwashed by picture tube. I feel
them up before I blossom boobs. Their thighs
so slick, I memorize. Sapphic, surreal,
vinyl eyes, adolescent alibis.

A dorm delivered living doll, my first
attempt, no alcohol. Long curly hair
and thigh high socks. Concerns of college/church
cast out, when our door locks, with underwear.

The shame, with age, a thing I just recall.
It's not a phase to love a babydoll.

THE CIMMERIAN

A sterling steeple, Cimmerian sky,
transfixing temple twinkle nigh. In clouds
charcoal your crucifix eclipse belies
anhedonia of atheists. Found
devotion beams below — recumbent peeks
a thousand flickers' glow. Wax heart, poured doll
dissolving urchin, urgent underneath
who tastes the sacrament of survival
with timid teeth. In radiance, beneath
her hollowing regrets evanescent
repentant child, adorned in ashen lace, wreath
drips fauna wild, her first dawn collected —
obeisance heathens never understand
that god is light — illuminated man.

CORNSEQUENCE

The spirit took your eyes away. They did
not blink once yesterday. Contemplation
a mirror lake, self reflection, morbid
mistake. Blind maternal insurrection.

A husk, your body, in cornfields, was grown
for children — brittle mommy/yellow corpse.
Cornsilk brunette, for meadow smiles alone,
the spirit takes your lips. It leaves remorse.

You did not know you were a sacrifice —
harvested hollow to play nice. Cracked skin
still scented of the wild — aroma vice.
The spirit takes the nose, last scents of sin.

A crafted warning is a cornhusk doll.
To love a child requires no face at all.

DOLLHOUSED

A cuckold made by babydoll, her throat
serrated, first reveal of claws. A man
she thought she could deceive. Demon dotes
a damsel, believed naive. A form human.
pretend, he takes. Reptilian heart, in half,
she breaks. A bloody gasp she thinks her last,
but no. Her torture down a tiny path
he shows. His shrunken siren he clasps
in palm, inside a dollhouse, with wrath,
embalmed. A three-inch sofa, minuscule
her tears, her pleas too teeny to meet
his ears. His fingers bring her close, so cruel,
a dangle, dump, diminutive defeat.
A hurt so big remade to something small
inside a house he crafts that's two-foot tall.

RAGDOLL

Remove what's rigid. Rules are bones. Leave veins
to bleed for him alone. Embalmed alive
red syrup treat. Your suffering remains
sticky sweet. Aftertaste, abuse survived,
a tinge of tragedy at five. You taste
the way a good girl should — smoked cherry seared,
his pyre pine, heartwood. Cutaneous
his cruelty, requisite flesh for tears
pretty. Unbuttoned eyes, black holes to stuff,
your flicker cotton candy snuffed. Wee ears,
for whispers, lips a crimson thread rebuffs.
Delivered limber in a limousine,
already broken, bent, by him, obscene.

KNOCKOFF DOLL

I'm in a corner of your mind. To mock,
undress, to use unkind. Not about me
much at all. Just recognize a knock-
off Barbie doll. A pink plastic beauty,
can I replace? I have that kind of fuck
me face. Not angular enough to be
name brand. Small town dime store bargain, a buck
you had on hand. Inadequately
long, limbs with dents, so hollow, cheap— careless
fingertip accidents. You've had the best.
You couldn't know how soon my shamefulness
would show. Impulse purchase, you should suppress.
Defective lesson in cut rate design
you designate a corner in your mind.

Four years old, love is cute & composed in pageant clothes,
rhinestoned crowned & posed, ruffles with white patent
bows, ten of the tiniest toes. Compassion is fashioned of blinky-eyed
plastic you ration since the days of ballet shoes with sewn-in peony
elastic on the feet of a Fozzie the Bear fanatic, polyester fur, a top
hat of plastic, demure, a duet, cheeks wet, an elementary school stage.
First friends are fibers -- plastic, polyester, elastic fantastic, but it's paper
that gets romantic, never pedantic, obscene, spring green pre-teen love.
In the noon of your life, you are a paper bloom. They give you the room,
the Puritans—even arm you with library cards to peruse stranger
bards on bookshelves. They don't insert themselves, silent as stars,
just credit cards, in the woods of Waldenbooks where stories on shelves
beseech on sight like lightning bugs in jars that light a night that
ends & you're all right. They visit the world of pretend -- book fairs,
fairytales, Saturday sales in neighborhood yards. Many not even hard,
but they tear apart your world as it was so far like it is just paper,
and your parents don't see it. You are on the brink. They let you slink
into this novel forest, feral homeland habitat, paperback page attack of
branched arms, cute fruit, a cover for a corpse of the tree it used
to be. They didn't see. Oppression oblivious to the indigenous
deciduous dangers of

INVISIBLE INK

in bindings, leather and weathered, onxy and pink are skeletons
dire, delicious, distinct. Best friends who wait above dolls,
post-mainstage & table dances, six hourly roll calls. They stay shut
on a shelf ready to mend. They open for you when you need to
transcend. So many collected, protected -- won't lend them to boys
who enjoy you and then disappear. Your body you'll give, but they
won't finger King Lear. These books become body, titles tattooed
dire, delicious, distinct. Nobody can see them but you. It's
your invisible ink.

CLUES

A girl detective, River Heights, as keen
on lockets, pearls as legal rights. You're robbed
a mother, three year's old. This jinx, a teen,
deciphers — never told. A turning knob
reveals a mystery. All they won't tell,
by candlelight you see. You speak in French
but not of loss. A roadster, blue pastel,
to house of moss. A missing clock, suspense —
what does it hide? Bank box details you find
inside. Accept no money for a case,
your pride, their pleasure a reward entwined,
that spider sapphire, rare, you can't replace.
A staircase secret seen through eyes ice blue;
in lilac, step through strife, collect your clues.

YOU KNOW YOU LOVE ME

Your island kingdom, thirteen miles, penthouse
princess, an Audrey smile. Tiara heart
by YSL, a maid a mother, blouse
Chanel. Your cappuccino counterpart,
serene scene stealer, rose gold tart, her gifts:
croissants, coffee, bone dry, no foam; her guilt:
atop his thighs, your boyfriend's moans. A rift
with sticks upon a hockey field, what's spilt
on steps, your reign and rage won't yield. Requires
a prince ruthless, ribald who makes you feel
seventeen years old — ignites fair flesh, pale fire
his own, your burlesque slips, a limo peel
to gramophone — two tamed by teen desire.
Each pout in Prada, Cornelia, I see.
I tell your tale, and you know you love me.

HOT PINK

Hot pink hydrangea tomb teenage, a cell
of swallowed bubblegum and rage. A door
I cannot lock to hide. A car they will
not allow me to drive. I'm stuck indoors
and in my head, but Henry Miller's in
my bed, abreast of Faulkner, Tennessee —
write harlots, captives, sad, like me. Girl friend
in ink Joyce Carol Oates, empathy,
erotic anecdotes. Next year eighteen,
if I survive, hot pink, full bloomed but half
alive. I do my time with the Marquis
de Sade. He sees my jailhouse virtue, laughs
"you fraud." Compatriots in sheets hot pink,
you wet your prison blossom, on the brink.

TRUE CRIME IN TREES

A book is nature, not good, evil, more
deciduous corpse of tree it used
to be. Stood 40 feet above & bore
its killers fruit, decade of shade, abused
by indifference, climbers fingers, feet
before the penetration of the blade.
The splintering skeleton bleats, creaks;
it's branches claw away, attempt to stay
another fleeting second inside sky.
A slice of life, majestic thud, the sound
of falling gods vivisected ghost we buy,
put high, some shelf, a dead animal bound
for dusty sacrifice. Forget to read.
Its story is the suffering of seeds.

DARKBLOOM

Night blossom, hawkish, witchy wiles, lovechild
in lightning with a pedophile. *My Cue,*
best book, biography. By art beguiled,
betrothed to Clare Quilty — dress black, ink blue.

Lolita floats inside kaleidoscope
of butterflies. Whim winged gleams, collector's
eyes. 12 year old on index cards. Captured
clippings, American bard, true predator.

LaSalle, pretender FBI, pre-teen thief,
a nickel shy, cross-country kidnap road
trip date, true criminal Humbert motif
1948; guilt's a glittered ode.

Nabokov still hides inside thorned dark blooms—
one anagram, two authors' tangled tomb.

ME

(For You, Caroline Kepnes)

Confession is a stack of books; such small
hands offer closer looks: mine Paula Cox
and Spaulding Gray — grad schoolgirl haul.
My nipples peek outside to play. Shoebox
apartment, windows wide, nude peepshow cuz
you're lurking outside. "I talk to strangers."
I tweet. Perform. My yellow stockings buzz,
and daddies swarm. Ivy urchin procured
by savant, street — you, bookstore cleric, judgment
replete. Bad mommy to a cracked cell phone,
writer who cannot be alone. You're sight,
so suddenly I'm seen — blue blood, brownstone,
pedagogically pristine. Twilight
bookstore benediction, your novel whore,
fingered pages devoured by a carnivore.

SEPULCHER

I'm bones beneath your buried breaths. Our vault
of ink bequeaths a dozen deaths. You cut
me in our currency. A shank, assault
syllabic, dissects veins emptied. Your slut
cadaver cannot shut you out. Through page,
our slab, you stroke a skeleton devout.
My sockets slick with sympathy. Your rage
a specter, sentient without pity.
It haunts in hostile homilies. Our grave:
redundant, symbiotic agonies.
The cruelest cuts, for books, we both shall save.
Our heat you heighten with hyperbole;
we're bound in leather for eternity.

Some girls get crowns, coordinating organza wedding gowns.
They settle down barbecues & babies, the Puritan pedigree of small
southern towns. Husbands have demons, Brooks Brothers bound,
seething, heavy breathing pushed deep & buttoned down. Behind three
piece suits suave & suppressed, they grind fangs behind pulpits, perverts
possessed, Sunday School pretenders in quaint paisley vests.
Side-eyes & secrets they pay a stripper in braids to divest.

Some girls get rings. The shine of reflected sanctimonious
sentiment stings. It slices through places inside you've sewn shut —
evisceration proliferation — a thousand platinum princess cuts.
They mean countless things, the gentility of gleams. The women who
wear them seem smug, sanctioned & safe. You're just entertainment,
an enjoyable toy of a waif. They empty wallets. They have some diamonds
for you, but they are strategically placed, so you won't misconstrue.

They give you

BRACELETS

some ornamentation that says you're craven & craved & a tart & taboo.
Inside them you're handcuffed, depraved. You do what you have to do to be okay.
They keep you in corners & cubbies prepared, a babydoll discreet, tucked away without
clothes, underwear. An aged nymphette they treat to cotton candy, ice cream.
They like your Hello Kitty pink sheets, doe-eyed sleepy innocent dreams. You're
sometimes locked tight in handcuffs, your profile is runaway. They'll let you
slip away shamefully soon. They have plans for today.

You feel criminal, subliminal, caged, on the side – a secret so shameful
they punish & hide. It feels normal to you in all the worst ways. You
know the scene & the dialogue. You've memorized your part in this play
since the debut performance, the true crime of your young life. You're
good in this role because a knife is a knife. It's not acting to feel. It cuts the
same way as it did five years old. They plunge it inside your own murdered child soul
(because when a man takes the tiny parts of you he has taken the whole.)

You're not a girl with a crown.
You're not a girl with a ring.
You get their bracelets & handcuffs.
You give them everything.

WHEN YOU ARE DROWNING IN A CAR

When you are drowning in a car, headlights
illuminate you piscine stars. Windshield
fishbowl, a brown/black sky. Midnight airtight,
three hours to die. Alone, stretched neck appeals,
air bubble breaths -- thirteen months you grieved
his brother's death. A blonde borrowed
from a boiler room. Black Oldsmobile, he leaves
you, a tomb. 30, you'd be tomorrow
and a week -- bobbing chin, passenger seat
When you are drowning in his car, do you
believe the curse? Can't breathe. No stars. Batique
scales, flat eyes float by tragedy see-through,
unempathetic view, your black bell jar,
just you alone and drowning in a car.

WHAT IS DEAD

Do you hear it — what is dead? Sibilance
in shrunken head. Asphyxiated, ice
cream truck, backmasked melodic Maypole dance
then self destruct. Sleepwalking sacrifice,
from edge of cliff to paradise. Each step
directed by a voice, eked eloquence —
edict, not choice. A scream between bicep
and bent elbow, all sound compressed
to muffled adagio. Drowns you out
like chloroform. Its prophesies you breathe,
conform. Become a girl, black lipstick pout
put on a wooden sable steed to grieve.
For flesh in feathers, fast asleep in bed,
you have been awakened to what is dead.

DON'T ASK ME

Don't ask me why I didn't run — against
my cheek a silver gun. My sister's sobs
are all I hear, another gun inside
that fear. Momentum only breaths and throbs.

Don't ask me why I got inside — a life
at stake that isn't mine. A gunpoint push
becomes a backseat crawl. Regret is rife.
All else becomes so small, huddled hush.

Don't think you know why I complied. The swing
of metal, taste of blood. His chide: "you'll die."
Don't question me at 25, the things
I did to stay alive — and I survived.

Unless you've faced the darkness and a gun,
don't tell me what you think I should have done.

BLEACH

You didn't really lie, that Christmas fête
she asks about the dye — a neighbor friend
who wants to judge and preach. You do not get
a golden girl with dye but bleach. So you pretend
it was the sun. You're not the only one.
They crown the blonde heads quicker than the brown.
Won't know regret, like you: "I could have won,"
a public smiling shame in evening gown.
A parent wants what's better for their child:
the waving winner, princess, sashed, that thrives.
A truth civilians will never reconcile.
You bleach away the pain when she is five.
It will not be the last time that you lied
How many days she cried before she died?

TETHERED

My neighborhood a peninsula, like
my state, is barely tethered to mainland.
Cracked gravel pavement, a calloused hitchhike
to 1950's cottages, wetlands,
rough hands, a bear who lingered in the bay,
a week but got away and a nine
year old who suffocated by what they say
was discipline: 300 pounds confines
a runaway, bed mattress, soiled diamonds
no sheets — outside nobody beats. A waif
in streets who smiled. We became her island.
Bike riding crush who never stopped or waved,
still passing her house — tethered to me by
the dead. Her crime scene we just occupy.

Like any juvenile, you suck at self-denial. Subsist
a while -- five years on Blowpops, pretzels, cocktail
olives & champagne, private dicks & public naked pain,
courtesan well trained. You stalk them, a hustler hunter baiting
prey inside a windowless cage, neon spectacles shaped like
the organ that beats in you filled with all the requisite shame &
rage. These sugar daddies used/reduced to nothing more than a
living wage (the way you see them more & more, not even
people the way you did, at times, before). It's easier for you
to push it down the feeling part – a heart swallowed quickly,
drowned like the now essential beginning-of-shift
lemon drop shot. The sting so hot you chase with sugar &
a Coke, the dirtiness perhaps not erased but cloaked the way
your skin is not.

And then one day, some prey who figures out he isn't ever
going to get that blowjob or threeway or girl show for which
he's perpetually pulling money from some reptilian wallet,
offering to pay, grabs, hard, tops of your two arms & shakes
until your teeth clang against each other. You bit your lip
as bouncers wrestle him efficiently away. He's made an
irreparable rip in your favorite crocheted sweater
you bought in the girl's department of a Target, fits a
10-12 year old, and you're 30. A winter purchase, and now
it's summer but perpetually fall & frigid inside a place where
erect nipples equal cash. Irreplaceable and it's trashed,
your lucky sweater, you wear in a year, the shape of your
breasts pulled yarn so darn seductive, the way it matches
exactly the shade of your skin fascinates so many men
but never again. You ask when does this stop? When you're 30,
like you once said, or when you are a past-your-prime pigtailed
joke who's broke or dead? When you must trade your amateur
status for professional begger in somebody's bed? Do you have
another year to find the perfect lucky crocheted sweater
and mold its cream colored pieces to hug the shape of
your chest, or is it time to resign, to let it fall?

The way he does, pushed by an ex-college linebacker
out a front door. You don't want this anymore, not
one more day. You let it fall because you know at heart you are

FEMME
FATALE

A womanchild is always young enough to learn to live another way.

GIRL IN A CAGE

The ransom written in her hand — some scrawl,
a smear of tears, demands, a film inside:
ten frames disgrace, a cage so small she crawls,
her dirty face — delivered by PI,
pinstripes, trench coat, half past midnight, a knock,
manila envelope to drowsy dad
who seethes in silk. Unlocks a safe well-stocked,
"Brutes won't be bilked." Briefcase he pads
half million bucks. "Pier Park, daybreak," the note
instructs. "Off Dock 1, dump and don't look back."
Beneath PI retrieves what fortune floats,
joins caged cohort upon his boat. "Unpack
it, pay me, set me free." His speech soft, sage:
"Don't see a partner, just girl in a cage.

SLUT SHAME

It's funny how they always blame it on
the girl. Cherchez la femme now slut shame. Like
itty bitty me could debase the sons
of industry and prep school breeding. Strike
some blow against the aristocracy
still armed with money, power even God
when I don't even have a solid plan,
decent reputation. Use my body
and blame me for your weakness. It can't be
you. It cannot be that I was something
so pettable you gave it all to see
me crawl across your kitchen nude and lean
like some malnourished kitty cat while you
hold all the milk and savor every mew.

KATE SPADE WALLET

Depression, black, the Kate Spade wallet pushed
down deep inside my Barbie pink Coach purse.
Its zipped, compressed plastic essentials, smushed
identity — an empty paper curse
of days in pocket, tainted currency
transacted from a toxic world. Two gifts
my mother gave me, the accessories
of womanhood for days when bodies lift
their skeletons from silk designer tombs
wear leather, pastel cheerfulness that masks
beneath lipstick, a cadaver exhumed
decomposing in sunlight while you bask.
When subterfuge of suffering is art,
you see just pink not the black, buried heart.

RUNAWAY

You're old enough to know how this will end.
Don't long for anyplace you've ever been.
Plane ride to an imaginary friend,
details so perfect he crafts with a pen.

Nothing's as romantic as far away.
Only a stranger can make you feel new.
His city the setting, lines you will say,
you're easily written, so he'll cast you.

A part you sink into; you even smile,
your hair and your body all his to convey.
You forget it's an act after a while.
Then some new director writes you a play.

How old must you be to learn how to stay?
Will you ever not want to runaway?

PYROGRAPHY

A glowing of tendrils, amber, iris
aflame, this pirouette, light in midnight,
once had a name. Mesmerized, one dark eye,
remnant of life, immolates, at first sight,
virgin, midwife. Reminder this kindling
once was alive. Difference extinguished
in smoke survives. They tell of your twinkling,
the height of your blaze. Porcelain ash
begets their perpetual haze. They can shake you
from hair, disseminate your heart. One eye
memorized, an iridescence tattoo —
biography inside pyrography.
You ended on oak. Their flicker remakes
a girl into fire transcending the stake.

GIRL WITH A PEN

A southern snowflake in blizzard descends.
The winter you're born beach town's snowed in.
An alabaster tourist never blends.
You're not like your parents. You don't pretend.

Your town's churches, strip clubs. Puritans sin.
You know very well by the time you're ten.
It's beaten inside 'til you comprehend.
Their notion of naked you will transcend.

They show their souls while you show them your skin.
Champagne room secrets, they let you listen.
Girl just beginning, they don't know your end.
You write, in pink ink, these businessmen.

It's who you become not how you begin.
How they will know you is girl with a pen.

Acknowledgements

Cheerotica was first published in *Pink Litter*.
Pink Plastic House was first published in *Anti-Heroin Chic*.
Broken Little Girls and *Domesticated Animus* was first published in *A Restricted View From Under the Hedge*.
You Don't Want This was first published in *Pink Litter*.
XXX TTY was first published in *SWWIM*.
Entertainers was first published in *Picaroon Poetry*.
Broom was first published in *Five: 2:*
Plaid Kitten, The Cimmerian was first published in *Rhythm & Bones*.
Unbound was first published in *Quail Bell Magazine*.
Talking To A Teenage Girl About Her Mouth and *An Entrance Is Not An Exit* were first published in *The Cerurove*.
14 and kneeling before a jv defensive line coach was first published in *8 Poems*.
Peepholes was first published in *Paper and Ink Girls To The Front*.
Nailbiter and *Experiment* were first published in *Rabid Oak*.
Your Husband Drives Me Home was first published in *Anti-Heroin Chic*.
Sock Slut was first published in *Pink Litter*.
Vortex was first published in *The Mystic Blue Review* in.
Hitchhiker was first published in *Speculative 66*.
Veruca Wants was first published in *Neologism Poetry Journal*.
Candy Cigarettes was first published in *Bone & Ink Press*.
Half of His Heart was first published in *Mojave Heart Review*.
Ambition was first published in *Anti-Heroin Chic*.
Red Licorice, Black Lingerie was first published in *Pink Litter*.
Blow Pop Love was first published in *Faded Out*.
Domesticated Animus was first published in *A Restricted View From Under the Hedge*.
Plastic Heads was first published in *Anti-Heroin Chic*.
Babydoll was first published in *Visitant Lit*.
Cornsequence was first published in *TERSE. Journal*.
Dollhoused was first published in *Water Soup*.
Ragdoll was first published in *Mookychick*.
Knockoff Doll and *Me* were first published in *Feminine Collective*.

Preditor was first published in *Glass: A Journal of Poetry*.
Primitive was first published in *Porridge Magazine*.
Even Assholes Get to be Anonymous and *True Crime In Trees* was first published in *The New Southern Fugitives*.
Lunar Math and *Bleach* were first published in *Mojave Heart Review*.
A Map of Pinecones was first published in *Anti-Heroin Chic*.
Kristins was first published in *Here Comes Everyone: The Brutal Issue*.
Good Girl Gone was first published in *Wanton Fuckery*.
Hot Pink was first published in *Tepid Autumn*.
Sepulcher was first published in *Neologism*.
What is Dead, Girl With A Pen & When You Are Drowning In A Car were first published in *Luna Luna Magazine*.
Don't Ask Me and *Darkbloom* were first published in *Feminine Collective*
Tethered was first published in *Mojave Heart Review*.
Girl in a Cage was first published in *Burning House Press*.
Slut Shame was first published in *Occulum*.
Kate Spade Wallet was first published in *Mookychick*.
Runaway was first published in *Murmur Journal*.
Pyrography was first published in *The Ginger Collect*.
It's Not Hard To Put A Stripper in Cuffs was first published in *Former Cactus*.
The Scarlet Socks was first published in *Pussy Magic*.
Your Body is His Blessing was first published in *Yes Poetry*.
Necropolis was first published in *Mookychick*.
Nipple was first published in *Mojave Heart Review*.
Kitten Smitten was first published in *Ghost City Review*.
Peeler, Chinatown and *Half-Finished Houses* were first published by *Tiny Flames Press*.
Stripping on 9/11 was first published by *Yes Poetry*.
Fishnet Noir was first published in *Sock Slut* by *Moonchaps*.
Kneesock Code was first published in *Sock Slut* by Moonchaps.

"In her debut full length collection of sonnets and prose poems, Kristin Garth will capture the very essence of your soul. Upon reading this tome, I was rendered speechless and without a flowing river of ink. The makers of aural pleasure will fall silent. The visual creators will stare at a blank canvas. All creators in the arts will cease what they are currently manifesting for but a moment to reflect on the very nature of darkness. The living embodiment of suffering lives and breathes poisonous oxygen in Garth's words and has added struggle as an unfortunate ally. The very aspect of not knowing if there is a route of escape at the ready can frighten any timorous being. Based on a rather turbulent time in Garth's life, her temporary light is shed on the direction of stripping. In doing so, she has taken on the persona of a schoolgirl. Beneath the guise of a smiling academic is a warrior who tried with all her might to unleash herself.

Her language is that of film noir. Think of jazz music from the late 1940s to the early 1950s while you are reading and picture the sleek and sly elements of femme fatales, people donning zoot suits, private dicks, and much more. Imagine taking a moonlit stroll through the streets of a city, where the only light reflects from the lamplight and the occasional brightly lit apartment. Split into different sections, *Candy Cigarette Womanchild Noir fused* sonnets and prose poems together in a way that no one has ever dared to attempt before. Two writing methods that often collide, one of great poetic value and one of spontaneous literary combustion, Garth has meticulously sought out the perfect message and has hidden it between the lines of these pieces. A confessional spirit from first syllable to last, the words embedded in this book are sure to alter your mindset. I have followed Garth's work since a few moments after the beginning and as I watched her escalate to her current zenith, I was not the least bit surprised.

The creative spark within her has been set ablaze and has matured to an inferno. From her inferno of words, this book and other chapbooks preceding this one took on lives of their own. Reading her work and demanding more is an addiction...and it is official. I am a Kristin Garth addict. Join me, won't you, fellow creators? Put on your best pair of knee-high socks and bury your exposed and vulnerable heart in the pages of *Candy Cigarette Womanchild Noir,* a must-have for any lover of contemporary poetry with a twist of Shakespearean cameos."

- Z.M. Wise: Poet